HAVANA

THE CITY AT A GLANCE

Teatro Nacional

Nicolás Arroyo and Gabriela Mené[...] building was finished in 1960 but only opened in 1979. Visit for the art-strewn lobby, and the top-floor bar's late-night gigs and iconic views.
Avenida Paseo y 39, T 879 6011

Ministerio de Relaciones Exteriores

The 1959 blue-glazed Foreign Ministry, by José Fontan and Carlos Ferrer, stares out to sea over the clam-shell roof of Estadio José Martí.
Calle Calzada 360 esq G

Edificio López Serrano

Ricardo Mira and Miguel Rosich designed the vertical shafts and ziggurats of this 1932 art deco hulk. Don't miss Enrique García Cabrera's nickel-silver *El Tiempo* relief in the vestibule.
Calle 13, 106 entre L y M

Edificio FOCSA

This mighty winged beast was once one of the world's largest reinforced concrete buildings. Yet from afar, it appears ready for take-off.
See p010

Tryp Habana Libre

Castro and Guevara moved into the new $24m hotel after Cuba fell. History absolved them.
See p028

Ministerio de Comunicaciones

Long after Che's face first graced this square (see p012), Camilo Cienfuegos showed up on the old postal HQ. The question on everyone's lips – how long before Fidel joins them?
Avenida Independencia esq Aranguren

Hospital Hermanos Ameijeiras

A bank turned into a hospital post-revolution, it still houses the national vault in its bowels.
See p014

INTRODUCTION

THE CHANGING FACE OF THE URBAN SCENE

Cuba today is like one of its blushing *quinceañeras*, a teenager on the cusp of freedom from an overbearing father. But how will she mature? Since Raúl Castro's succession, change is afoot. To counter state job cuts, half a million self-employment licences have been issued, and the legalisation of ventures that attract the hallowed tourist dollar has created a small but previously unheard-of middle class (of some 200 sanctioned professions, palm-tree pruner and 'dandy' have had less impact). Foreign investment is being courted, through golf resorts that would have been reappropriated in times gone by, and, more poignantly, in a Brazilian-financed mega-port and special economic zone in Mariel, west Havana, from where so many Cubans once floated away. Now they return from Miami by air, with much-needed hardware, iPhones and pockets full of cash.

As the country opens up, the fear is that the greenbacks and blue eyes will corrupt. Havana is unique in that its original architecture is intact – each district is a showcase of the *en vogue* styles of its era. The colonial core is being restored but the rest of the city is in dire need of protection. At least living in a bubble has shielded it from common Latino afflictions. It has no shanty towns and little crime, and its well-educated citizens have a social sensibility embodied in Raúl's daughter, a champion of gay rights. But change happens slowly here and is often a chimera. Habaneros shrug, and reason that while they wait, they may as well face the music and dance.

ESSENTIAL INFO

FACTS, FIGURES AND USEFUL ADDRESSES

TOURIST OFFICE
Infotur
Obispo 524 entre Bernaza y Villegas
T 866 3333
www.infotur.cu

TRANSPORT
Car hire
Rex
T 835 6830
www.rex.cu
Transtur
T 835 0000
www.transtur.cu
Taxis
CubaTaxi
T 855 5555
Almost every car on the street is a potential taxi; official ones have blue number plates

EMERGENCY SERVICES
Ambulance
T 104
Fire
T 105
Police
T 106
Late-night pharmacy (until 8pm)
Farmacia Internacional Miramar
Avenida 41 esq 20
T 204 4350

EMBASSIES AND CONSULATES
British Embassy
Calle 34, 702-704 esq 7ma
T 214 2200
www.ukincuba.fco.gov.uk
US Interests Section
Swiss Embassy
Calzada entre L y M
T 833 3551
havana.usint.gov

POSTAL SERVICES
Post office
Oficios 102 entre Lamparilla y Amargura
Shipping
DHL
Avenida 1ra y 26
T 204 1876

BOOKS
Dirty Havana Trilogy by Pedro Juan Gutiérrez (Faber & Faber)
Great Houses of Havana by Hermes Mallea (Monacelli Press)
Revolution of Forms: Cuba's Forgotten Art Schools by John A Loomis (Princeton Architectural Press)

WEBSITES
Art/Culture
www.cnap.cult.cu
www.cubarte-english.cult.cu
Magazines
www.cubaabsolutely.com
www.havanatimes.org

EVENTS
La Bienal de La Habana
www.bienalhabana.cult.cu
Festival of New Latin American Cinema
www.habanafilmfestival.com

COST OF LIVING
Taxi from José Martí Airport to Vedado
CUC25
Cappuccino
CUC2.5
Packet of cigarettes
CUC3
Daily newspaper
MN0.20
Bottle of champagne
CUC40

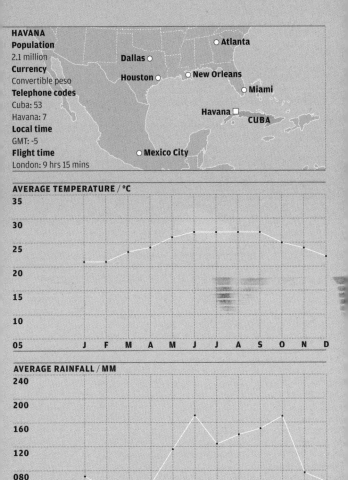

HAVANA
Population
2.1 million
Currency
Convertible peso
Telephone codes
Cuba: 53
Havana: 7
Local time
GMT: -5
Flight time
London: 9 hrs 15 mins

Atlanta
Dallas
Houston New Orleans
Miami
Havana
CUBA
Mexico City

AVERAGE TEMPERATURE / °C

```
35
30
25
20
15
10
05
    J  F  M  A  M  J  J  A  S  O  N  D
```

AVERAGE RAINFALL / MM

```
240
200
160
120
080
040
000
    J  F  M  A  M  J  J  A  S  O  N  D
```

NEIGHBOURHOODS

THE AREAS YOU NEED TO KNOW AND WHY

To help you navigate the city, we've chosen the most interesting districts (see the map inside the back cover) and underlined featured venues in colour, according to their location (see below); those venues that are outside these areas are not coloured.

PLAZA DE LA REVOLUCIÓN

This monumental expanse, built to impress in the 1950s by dictator Fulgencio Batista, was commandeered by Castro for the same purpose. It's loosely enclosed by ministries, cultural venues and an obelisk memorial to José Martí (see p015), who is as much a revolutionary hero as the two 'C's. Among all this puffed-out-chest architecture are sweet touches of everyday life, such as the musicians practising among the trees.

MIRAMAR

The first bridge across the Río Almendares was finished in 1910, and by the 1940s the rich were moving west to build mansions along the wide avenues. It's still well-off. Restaurants like La Fontana (Calle 3ra esq 46, T 202 8337) attract diplomats, foreign businessmen and the in-crowd. Also check out the delightful La Esperanza (Calle 16, 105 entre 1ra y 3ra, T 202 4361) and hip nightspots such as Espacios (see p053).

HABANA VIEJA

In 1519, the city was founded here, and the unique melange of colonial architecture became a World Heritage Site in 1982. It's a mix of baroque, Moorish and art nouveau flourish that is half ruined, half restored. In the early evening, main drag Obispo is a riot of bars, live music, shops and hustlers ('Oye, amigo, where you fron?'), and Plaza Vieja has been returned to its former glory. Yet, off the beaten path, crumbling facades are kept up by makeshift wooden beams.

LA RAMPA

Rising from the Hotel Nacional (see p020) to ice-cream palace Coppelia (see p039), La Rampa was the hub of 1950s cavorting and is still a strut for locals of all persuasions. It bustles with offices, shops, cafés, cinemas (see p074) and matinee clubs. La Zorra y El Cuervo (La Rampa entre N y O, T 833 2402) is an intimate jazz den, and the cocktails and posh burgers at Waoo!!! (Calle L y 25, T 832 8424) are the perfect fit for the area.

VEDADO

After the sugar price spiked due to WWI, the bourgeoisie built their homes here in Italianate and neoclassical styles, with gardens, fountains and sculptures – the Museo de Artes Decorativas (see p068) is a superb example. Later decades saw the arrival of the art deco Casa de las Américas (see p072) and the 1950s Hotel Riviera (see p026). It's a cultured, tranquil part of the city, with theatres, museums and parks.

CENTRO

Havana's heart is a dense jumble of lost elegance and lives played out in public, and by night its unlit streets are other-worldly. The 1927 Compañía Cubana de Teléfonos (Aguila 565) is a terracotta-iced confection next to Chinatown, while Parque Central is ringed by hotels; the 1915 Gran Teatro (Paseo de Martí 458, T 861 3077), home to the ballet; and the Capitolio (see p009). Grand old El Prado, centre of the nascent housing market, shuffles down to the sea.

LANDMARKS

THE SHAPE OF THE CITY SKYLINE

The best way to get a handle on Havana is to brave the rickety lifts of the 123m Edificio FOCSA (overleaf) or the 113m Memorial José Martí (see p015). From these two lookouts you see a city virtually unaltered since 1959. The lack of modern skyscrapers does mean that the few high rises that do exist stand out on the flat skyline, which is useful, as asking locals for directions is generally fruitless. Dominating Parque Central is the 91m dome of the incongruous 1929 Capitolio Nacional (Industria y Barcelona). Built on US credit and always seen as an imperialist folly, it is being renovated to surprisingly house the Cuban National Assembly. Elsewhere, the Habana Libre (see p028) rises above La Rampa; the giant, striped Meliá Cohiba (see p016) signals the Vedado seafront; and the Embajada de Rusia (see p011) is the unloved beacon of Miramar.

Another useful anchor is the hub of Plaza de la Revolución, a mammoth town-planning initiative of the early 1950s, from which boulevards fan out to all corners. This was only the first stage of urban development – Castro's arrival in Havana actually preserved the city, as a 1956 proposal by famed Catalan architect Josép Lluís Sert, among other plans yet more radical, advocated razing the axes of Habana Vieja to replace them with tower blocks. In fact, so little has changed in half a century that today Havana is as much about its crumbling architecture as those who have to live with it. *For full addresses, see Resources.*

Edificio FOCSA

The 33 floors of Cuba's tallest residential structure went up in 1956. It was designed in a bird-in-flight shape by Ernesto Gómez Sampera and Martín Domínguez, and the Corbusian plans included a cinema, TV studios, offices and a pool. There was little consideration of the urban context in those heady times, as is seen in the foreground, where two eclectic-style mansions, one of which houses El Gato Tuerto (T 838 2696),

an intimate bolero haunt, are dwarfed by the green concrete giant. Post-revolution, many of FOCSA's privileged residents fled; its pool has lain empty for decades and has hosted many an impromptu baseball game. However, top-floor restaurant/bar La Torre (T 838 3089) remains one of the city's most upmarket old-school venues, so long as the elevator happens to be working. *Calle 17 entre M y N*

Embajada de Rusia

The 20-storey tower of the 1985 Russian Embassy is a striking, if sinister, triumph of ideologically charged architecture by Alexander Rochegov. The concrete-and-glass complex thrusts above the mansions of Miramar, converted into consulates and government offices post-revolution. As if a one-fingered salute to the USA across the water, the embassy's unique melodrama evokes the space race. It was once home to hundreds of Soviet comrades, but now little is left of their legacy, save the stretch Ladas bouncing over the city's potholes. These days a skeleton staff rattles around inside, with time to skid across the marble and contemplate Lenin set in stained glass, as well as murals by Rochegov's daughter, Anna. Like so much of Havana, it is a poignant reminder of Cuba's lost history.

Avenida 5ta, 6402 entre 62 y 66

Ministerio del Interior

This 1953 building by Aquiles Capablanca, clad in Jaimanitas stone and brise-soleil, and with a ceramic mural by Amelia Peláez, is the most successful in the Plaza de la Revolución. But the Ministry of the Interior only achieved tourist-trap status with the 1993 addition of a 30m frieze of old boss Che to the concave elevator block. Based on the 1960 Alberto Korda photo, flesh was made steel behind the spot where Castro gave a speech after Guevara was killed in 1967. It carries the slogan *Hasta la Victoria Siempre* and lights up at night. In 2009, Guevara was joined by fellow hero Camilo, who adorns Ernesto Gómez Sampera's 1954 Ministerio de Comunicaciones. Despite also being designed by sculptor Enrique Ávila, the craftsmanship is less accomplished and he appears rather cartoon-like – perhaps symbolic of the current state of the revolutionary ideals.
Avenida Céspedes esq Aranguren

Hospital Hermanos Ameijeiras

The largest hospital in Cuba sticks out like a sore thumb in low-rise Centro. The 23-storey winged tower of yellowy Jaimanitas stone and the expansive plaza overlooking the Malecón suggest big bucks, and indeed construction began under Batista when it was intended to be the National Bank, with the lobby housing a stock exchange. Post-revolution, it was decided that the unfinished building should provide a more worthy purpose. Original architect Nicolás Quintana was forced to leave the country in 1960 after falling out with bank president Guevara over plans that he considered to be impractical for a hospital, and latterly called it a 'crude hybrid'. It was eventually inaugurated in 1982 with the best facilities on the island, yet the archaic US embargo has resulted in a chronic lack of medicine.
San Lázaro y Belascoaín

Memorial José Martí

This tribute to Cuba's spiritual godfather is the centrepiece of Plaza de la Revolución's monumental symbolism. The star-shaped grey marble spire is deceptively tall (141m with spike) and you can see for 60km from the top – not *quite* as far as the relatives in Miami. Architect Aquiles Maza and sculptor Juan José Sicre won the competition for its design, but after Batista came to power he commissioned third-placed Enrique Luis Varela, his political crony. An outcry led to the addition of Sicre's 18m statue at its base. Construction began in 1953, the centenary of Martí's birth, and took five years. Behind it is the Communist Party HQ, in the 1957 Palacio de Justicia, ironically an Italian fascist-style design by José Pérez Benitoa & Sons. The vast plaza itself is used for political rallies and papal visits.
Avenida Paseo y Independencia

HOTELS

WHERE TO STAY AND WHICH ROOMS TO BOOK

Cuba embraced tourism as its cash cow, and a raft of ramshackle colonial properties have been reborn as boutiquey, often themed, hotels with staff who, unusually for state businesses, don't look as if they'd rather pull teeth. It's hard to fault Santa Isabel (Baratillo 9, T 860 8201), located in a 1784 residence in the Plaza de Armas, San Felipe (opposite), Saratoga (see p021) and, for sheer value for money, Hostal Valencia (Oficios 53 esq Obrapía, T 867 1037).

After Batista's 1955 tax incentives, mob-financed casino hotels shot up in Vedado, including the Riviera (see p026) and the Capri (Calle 21 esq N, T 833 3747), which reopened in 2014. The glamour has long gone, but their public spaces are wonderfully evocative. Business-oriented hotels like the Meliá Cohiba (Avenida Paseo entre 1ra y 3ra, T 833 3636) and Parque Central (Neptuno esq Zulueta, T 860 6627) have the wi-fi and all the facilities, but their sterility robs you of the Cuban experience, be that good or bad. As for the Miramar resorts, leave them in their seafront car parks.

Considering the parlous state of the economy, prices are high. Yet downgrade at your peril, as cheap-hotel publicity boasts of clothes hangers and clock radios. Better to take a room in a Cuban home, or *casa particular* – www.havanacasaparticular.com and www.cubacasas.net have a burgeoning selection (see p024). The experience is authentic, rewarding and a genuine help to locals. *For full addresses and room rates, see Resources.*

Palacio del Marqués de San Felipe

In a departure for government restoration arm Habaguanex, the interiors of this late 18th-century baroque palace are largely contemporary, as opposed to reproduction colonial. If you feel short-changed by this architectural mash-up delivered by Havana firm Proyecto Espacios and more than 40 local artisans, you'll be convinced once you step inside one of the 27 rooms. Three spacious suites are unlike anything seen before in Habana Vieja, with stand-alone jacuzzis, art-nouveau stylings and mod cons. Common areas showcase Cuban art, which can be admired from boxy furniture. A terrace overlooks the (now busy again) cruise-ship dock and the baroque 1738 San Francisco de Asís church, which hosts choral and chamber-music concerts. *Oficios 152 esq Amargura, T 864 9191, www.hotelmarquesdesanfelipe.com*

Hotel Terral

Not only is this Habaguanex's first purpose-built hotel, but it is part of its widening of focus from Habana Vieja to the prime real estate along the Malecón. The Jaimanitas stone block inserted into an empty plot beside the old Palacio Sarra (which is also being turned into a hotel) opened in 2012 and stands out for its taupe *mallorquinas* shutters, which protect against hurricanes, on the balconies of the 12 rooms. Proyecto Espacios' clean, modern interiors feature a four-storey 3D 'mural' (opposite), dark beech furniture, geometric stained glass and nature photography by Carlos Otero. The lobby/dining area is a tad squashed but it's the two Junior Suites (401, above) with expansive terraces on the roof that truly embrace this unbeatable location. *Malecón esq Lealtad, T 860 2100, www.habaguanexhotels.com*

Hotel Nacional de Cuba

The bunkers of this 1930 icon perched on a cliff facing Florida assumed strategic importance in the fraught Cuban Missile Crisis. New York firm McKim, Mead & White's conflation of art deco, neoclassical and neocolonial incorporates local marble, Jaimanitas stone and clay tiles. Interiors impress the moment you enter the lobby (above), which has coffered wood ceilings, Sevillan mosaics, chandeliers and iron-grille lifts. However, the Nacional's 457-room bulk hasn't been able to move with the times, and has sold out to the tour groups. That does mean the food is of high quality, notably in the Comedor de Aguiar, provided you are not put off by Michael Keaton's face on the menu. Have a nightcap in the cloisters – the bar is open very late. *Calle O esq 21, T 836 3564, www.hotelnacionaldecuba.com*

Hotel Saratoga

For luxury and convenience, Saratoga is the best place to stay in town. The eclectic neoclassical shell dates from the 1880s, and the hotel was a high-society haunt in the 1930s. It was remodelled and reopened in 2005 with two extra floors, reproduction features and an atrium that houses a palm-bedecked bar with a mural by Juan Carlos Botello. There are 96 rooms – Junior Suites face Parque Central – but for sheer style,

book the 100 sq m Habana Suite (above), with its Cuban marble and mahogany, claw-foot bath, shuttered windows and wraparound balconies. Service here is European standard, there's satellite TV, wi-fi, a small gym and spa area, and the rooftop pool/terrace (overleaf) has an eye-level view of the Capitolio dome. *Prado 603 esq Dragones, T 868 1000, www.hotel-saratoga.com*

Rooftop pool and terrace, Hotel Saratoga

Villa María

Cuba's unique economic model deserves credit for the rise of the global sharing culture, from Airbnb to pop-up restaurants. When *casas particulares* were legalised in 1997, Cubans simply rented out the granny room or bumped the kids. These days you can luxuriate in a 1950s Vedado penthouse at Artedel (T 830 8727) and, since 2010, even get the keys to your own apartment or villa. Many properties have a superb architectural pedigree, prices compare to those at the top hotels and, if you want creature comforts, simply employ a chef or chauffeur. Villa María (aka Villa Farah) is a covetable 1940 six-bedroom mansion set above the mouth of the Río Almendares, with minimal interiors, a kidney-shaped pool and a built-in bar. The gorgeous sweep of the two-storey balustraded staircase deservedly has star billing. Rent the whole house (families only) or one of the rooms. *T 362 0667, www.havanacasaparticular.com*

Hotel Riviera

Miami's Polevitzky, Johnson & Associates excelled with this seafront pleasure palace – the gambling mecca of mobster Meyer Lansky. The ceramic-clad dome housed the casino, its acoustics designed to augment the tempting sound of clattering chips. It's now used for bingo conventions and the like, but otherwise hotel interiors are little changed since Ginger Rogers sang on opening night in 1957. The low-slung lobby (pictured), with its swathes of marble, intricate wooden latticework, truncated staircase and sculptures by Cuban Florencio Gelabert and Italian Enzo Gallo, is a mini-museum. Unfortunately the same could be said for the 352 outdated rooms (Lansky stayed in 1923-24). Come for a martini in the bar. *Avenida Paseo y Malecón, T 836 4051, www.hotelhavanariviera.com*

Tryp Habana Libre

Welton Becket & Associates' modernist landmark at the top of La Rampa looms 125m above street level. It made a strong statement of capitalist intent in 1958, but Castro turned the tables 10 months later, when he chose the Presidential Suite La Castellana as his HQ in the early months of the revolution; ask at reception for a tour. Much altered but still relevant today, the Libre is buzzy and hip with a Latino clientele. The best of the 572 rooms are the highest – recessed balconies look out on the ocean or pool. The 25th-floor Turquino club has a retractable roof for salsa under the stars, there's a take on Morris Lapidus in the lobby (above) with its skylighted dome, and Amelia Peláez's mural on the plinth is now a symbol of the entire city.
Calle L esq 23, T 834 6100,
www.meliacuba.com

Hotel Florida

Perhaps the most accomplished of Habana Vieja's renovations, Florida is in the thick of the Obispo melee, but settle into a wicker chair in its two-tiered, porticoed atrium and calm descends. The 1836 noble-family residence retains an elegant intimacy. There are 25 spacious, colonial-style rooms that have wrought-iron beds and furnishings, high-beamed ceilings, blue-and-white porcelain, and checked Italian marble floors. Request the corner Suite 18 for its large balcony. The Piano Bar is one of the few venues in this part of town that is open late. Upholding the city's fine lobby tradition, the nearby art nouveau Hotel Raquel (T 860 8280) has a massive stained-glass skylight; top-floor Junior Suites here are the best keys. *Obispo 252 esq Cuba, T 862 4127, www.hotelfloridahavana.com*

Torre Atlantic penthouses

If concrete proof were still needed of the inexorable shift in government policy, this 2006 tower on the Malecón is it. Drinkers on the sea wall must have thought they'd had one too many rums as it went up – as nothing had happened here architecturally for decades. Designed by Maurizio Fantoni, it was financed by the Italian developers Bizzi & Partners. The lower volume houses a supermarket and pharmacy, and the cantilevered tower contains 96 flats, half of which were given to the government in the construction deal. There are two four-bedroom penthouses for rent, pimped-out with every amenity, including jacuzzis and a pool. It's the only option if you're in town to cut an album. All-white interiors feature Italian marble, ceramics and woodwork, and contemporary Cuban art.
T 833 0081, www.rentincuba.com

24 HOURS

SEE THE BEST OF THE CITY IN JUST ONE DAY

Many a soul has spent a whole 24 hours in Havana partying (yes *you*, Hemingway) and abstinence is nigh-on impossible. It's equally easy to achieve nothing – Cubans have made an art form of it – yet you need to be organised, as the top restaurants require a booking and 'official' business invariably takes an eternity, even buying ice cream at Coppelia (see p039). In addition, the architectural sights such as those in fascinating Centro (see p071), and the Cementerio (see p070) and art schools (see p076), are strung out, although it's possible to reach most on an open-top tourist bus, could you bear the shame. If you hail a taxi, don't count on the driver having the faintest idea where he's going – he's probably a nuclear engineer.

Cultural life is one thing that's rich in Cuba. Exhibitions and gigs, often last-minute or off-the-cuff, take place in all types of venues, including arts clubs Teatro Bertolt Brecht (see p040) and Hurón Azul (UNEAC, Calle 17 esq H, T 832 4551), so ask around to find *la cosa buena*. You'll already be aware of the old-time musicians but look out for the new generation – singers Eme Alfonso (see p062), Danay Suárez and Diana Fuentes, pianists Harold López-Nussa and Roberto Fonseca, Descemer Bueno (fusion), Ogguere (hip hop), Charanga Habanera (timba) and Gente de Zona (reggaeton).

And remember that if you encounter any obstacles in Havana, even a modest *propina* (tip) will get you an extremely long way. *For full addresses, see Resources.*

10.00 Museo Nacional de Bellas Artes

After breakfast with a view in La Torre del Oro (T 860 8560) on the ninth floor of the neo-Moorish Sevilla Hotel, cross the road to the country's best collection of Cuban art, housed in a modernist block designed by Alfonso Rodríguez Pichardo. It opened in 1954 and is an exemplar of the synthesis of art and architecture that Latin America does so well, with sculpture by Rita Longa at the entrance and balconies containing pieces by Mateo Torriente, Teodoro Ramos Blanco and Ernesto González. An internal patio (above) references the colonial tradition. Art is displayed chronologically: look for Carlos Enrique's *El Rapto de las Mulatas*, Wifredo Lam's *Maternidad* and Victor Manuel García's *Gitana Tropical* (the Cuban *Mona Lisa*). Closed Mondays. *Trocadero entre Monserrate y Zulueta, T 863 2118, www.museonacional.cult.cu*

11.30 Museo de la Revolución

You can't escape politics in Cuba, so get up to speed with the exhaustive displays inside the 1919 former Presidential Palace, a riot of classical allusions and Spanish revival overtones by Rodolfo Maruri and Belgian Paul Belau. The Salón de los Espejos (Hall of Mirrors; above) was used for lavish state receptions and has interiors by Tiffany & Co, as well as an enormous ceiling painting by Cuban Armando Menocal. Engaging exhibits include the tiny suit of astronaut Arnaldo Tamayo Méndez (the first Latino in space). Fidel Castro's ex-security chief claimed there were 638 attempts on his life, and some hapless, Bond-style CIA plots are revelled in, from exploding cigars to a poisoned wetsuit, as well as shoe polish meant to make Castro's distinctive beard fall out, destroying his power, à la Samson. *Refugio 1 esq Misiones, T 862 4098*

12.45 Real Fábrica de Tabacos Partagás
Peddling cigars (and whatever your heart desires) is a full-time job for Habana Vieja's street-corner characters but it's advisable to buy direct. The Partagás factory was founded in 1845 and its colourful facade and decorative roof are located behind the Capitolio. It produces 12 million *puros* a year, most of which are made by hand, each worker specialising in a specific *vitola* (size). Brands such as Montecristo and Cohiba complement Partagás' range, which has a dense, earthy taste – the unique Culebra (snake) is three cigars intertwined. A *lector* still reads the papers to the 400 employees but, sadly, cigars are not rolled on the thighs of virgins. Whether that was just an urban myth, or the city simply ran out of them, remains a mystery. Tours will resume in late 2014 after restoration.
Industria 520 esq Dragones

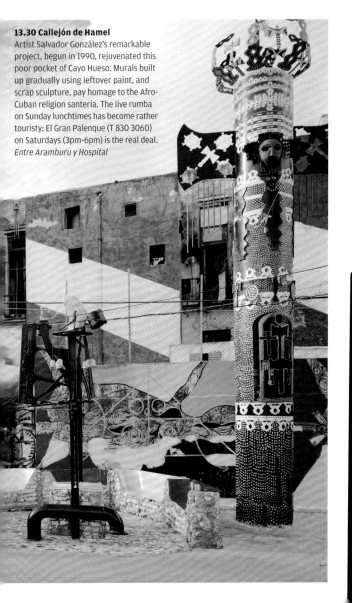

13.30 Callejón de Hamel
Artist Salvador González's remarkable project, begun in 1990, rejuvenated this poor pocket of Cayo Hueso. Murals built up gradually using leftover paint, and scrap sculpture, pay homage to the Afro-Cuban religion santeria. The live rumba on Sunday lunchtimes has become rather touristy; El Gran Palenque (T 830 3060) on Saturdays (3pm-6pm) is the real deal.
Entre Aramburu y Hospital

14.00 Café Laurent

This slick operation occupies a fifth-floor penthouse of a typical 1950s Vedado block, designed by Alberto Prieto. The layout has barely altered, from the curved corners to the home cocktail bar, which makes it even more fascinating – a bedroom is now a private dining space and the bathroom is exactly that. There's a cream and brown palette, period furniture and a wall covered with pages from 1950s kitchen design magazines. Chef Dayron Ávila Alfonso has worked in San Sebastián and it shows in the skilful execution of more than 30 dishes (seafood is a speciality). Dine on the lovely terrace, which has a great view of Edificio López Serrano. A word of warning – get out of the lift on the wrong floor and you'll walk straight into someone's apartment.
Calle M 257 entre 19 y 21, T 832 6890, www.cafelaurentcuba.com

15.30 Coppelia

The ice cream sold here is one of few post-revolution luxuries, Castro's let-them-eat-cake gift to the people. The 1966 vaulted concrete pavilion, designed by Italian Mario Girona and engineer Maximiliano Isoba, resembles something out of *The Jetsons*. Its spidery arms form outdoor enclosures shaded by banyan trees, and the upper level (above) is sectioned off with wood and coloured glass. There's space for 1,000, yet still there are queues for the day's flavours; it's an unmissable slice of urban theatre. Foreigners are corralled towards a CUC van, but it's easy enough to sneak in at the side (prices are in local pesos). Closed Mondays. Over the road is Cine Yara, part of Junco, Gastón and Domínguez's 1947 Radiocentro complex, now a weekend date venue for teens and a gay rendezvous. *Calle 23 y L*

16.30 Teatro Bertolt Brecht

Such was architect Aquiles Capablanca's considered approach to the Hebrew Centre, built on a corner site in the mid-1950s, he gave it two completely different faces. On the west facade, offices are protected by brise-soleil, and the synagogue (opposite) is encased in concrete and fronted by an empty volume that supports a hyperbolic arch. It's a private space, yet floating stairs are glimpsed through the glazing.

The north (above) is far more open, and a ramp leads to an auditorium with recessed terraces. This half was bought by the state in 1981 and now functions as a theatre. Below it, the low-ceilinged basement Café Brecht is the centre of a happening scene, hosting gigs by top contemporary acts such as Síntesis and Interactivo on its circular stage. Swing by to see who's playing later. *Calle 13 esq I, T 832 9359*

17.30 Plaza de la Catedral

The ornate fossilised coral facade of the baroque cathedral, which was finished in 1777, and two 18th-century palaces provide the backdrop to this enchanting square. It looks spectacular lit up at night when concerts are often staged. On the way here, stroll down lively Obispo, where music blares out of every door. La Lluvia del Oro (T 862 9870) has live salsa and a long art deco mahogany bar.

18.30 Malecón

Dusk signals a migration to the seafront promenade, and all aspects of Cuban life are acted out here over countless bottles of rum, on 'the longest sofa in the world'. As a social space it is far from homogeneous, each stretch having its conventions. Sea defences were crucial to the development of Havana, considering its regular buffeting by hurricanes. US engineers Mead and Whitney began the Malecón in 1901 at Castillo de la Punta and progress inched along, reaching La Rampa in 1923 and the Río Almendares in 1959 to link with the new Miramar tunnel. The porticoed buildings lining the Centro stretch have been ravaged by erosion. A few are now being restored and, where they have collapsed entirely, interventions include a stylish hotel (see p018) and Proyecto Espacios' pop-up tapas bar Lava Día on the corner of Manrique.

21.00 Casa Miglis

Gregarious Swede Michel Miglis has worked in Cuban film and pop for decades, and with designer Andreas Hegert he has devised an inspired mash-up here. The restaurant has a loose Gustavian style that melds with the original 1922 tiles and high ceiling. Classic Swedish design such as the Ericofon is framed on walls (even IKEA gets a look-in) and used as tableware, and the surprising menu features meatballs, lingonberries and local fish. The bar attests to Cuban ingenuity, from the 1950s carved counter to the recycled chairs mounted on pipes, creating high stools. A back patio and hall host DJs, jazz bands and, often, weekend parties. If the kitchen is closed as a result, the famously photogenic La Guarida (T 866 9047) is nearby, but come here for afters. *Lealtad 120 entre Ánimas y Laguna, T 864 1486, www.casamiglis.com*

23.30 Casa de la Música Galiano

Since 1941, the lexicon of Cuban music has graced this showbiz palace. The immense art deco América Building was designed as a residential and entertainment complex (inspired by Radio City in New York) by Fernando Martínez Campos and Pascual de Rojas. The variety theatre's zodiac-motif lobby floor, split double staircase and leather-upholstered anterooms are period pieces, but the dancefloor action is next door in Casa de la Música (above), which puts on live salsa and timba from the likes of Los Van Van; regular matinees featuring cubaton are mobbed by locals. Classic label Egrem also runs the touristy sister venue in Miramar (T 204 0447) and holds acoustic gigs at Areito Patio-Bar (T 862 0673; 5pm-7pm, Wednesday to Saturday), outside the studios in which Buena Vista recorded.
Galiano 267, T 862 4165, www.egrem.com.cu

URBAN LIFE
CAFÉS, RESTAURANTS, BARS AND NIGHTCLUBS

Cuban cuisine has long had a bad reputation as low set wages ate away at any incentive to please diners. Yet that old joke: 'What are the three failures of the revolution? Breakfast, lunch and dinner' is no longer relevant, as the grassroots *paladares* based in people's homes laid to rest the ghost of bland *ropa vieja* (the national dish, literally 'old clothes'). Since 2011, the fussy bureaucracy has been further relaxed and now you can feast like a king, or a government crony at least, in a neocolonial mansion (opposite) or a modernist villa (see p058). Although there have always been a few top-end state establishments – El Tocororo (Calle 18 entre 3ra y 5ta, T 204 2209) serves wild boar and ostrich and has a hip bar – Raúl has taken a leap of faith by leasing premises to entrepreneurs. Tomás Erasmo, who often cooked for the Castros, now presents peerless creole dishes in his homely Mama Inés (Obrapía 60, T 862 2669).

The cutting-edge music and nightlife scene happens in off-the-radar dives and large suburban restaurants that segue into outdoor clubs. Anywhere with a pool is popular. A mythical info line lists the night's action – good luck with that as the number regularly changes. One thing that never will is Cabaret Tropicana (Calle 72, 4505, T 267 1717). It's a CUC100 sting, but Max Borges Recio's 1951 telescopic vaults are a triumph of function and location. So you've come for the architecture, not the skimpy costumes, right? Right? *For full addresses, see Resources.*

Atelier

This was the first *paladar* since the singular La Guarida (see p046) to truly show what could be achieved. The late 18th-century mahogany-roofed villa, once owned by a senator, was acquired in a house swap and opened as Atelier in 2010, helped by its proximity to two big hotels but never losing sight of the detail. Antique furniture and heirlooms pique the interest; large, well-spaced tables are laid with 1950s crockery and Murano glassware; and walls hung with striking canvases by René Peña (above) and Moisés Finalé. From the daily menus written on stock-take slips, prawns are done eight ways and the rabbit and duck are legendary. After dinner, chilled tunes and a sea breeze waft over a series of terraces, exuding an Ibiza-esque vibe. *Calle 5ta, 511 altos, entre Paseo y 2, T 836 2025, www.atelier-cuba.com*

Le Chansonnier

The second incarnation of Héctor Higuera's renowned Le Chansonnier is located in an elegant neoclassical mansion. Times have changed since the original got entangled in red tape – *paladares* can now even buy wholesale. Yet early mornings still see legions of staff on frantic market sweeps, as one will have only oranges and another no onions, or the lorry carrying the eggs hit a pothole. Meanwhile, owners petition Cuba-bound contacts to stuff suitcases with spices. You'd never know it to taste the octopus carpaccio, or duck in olives, from the Frenchified menu here. Interiors match the kitchen's ambition. Bathrooms are camouflaged within Damián Aquiles' scrap-metal installation (above), and the edgy photography and painting is for sale. *Calle J 257 entre 15 y Línea, T 832 1576, www.lechansonnierhabana.com*

Café Madrigal

Filmmaker Rafael Rosales' fascinating home is crammed with the paraphernalia of 20 years in Cuban cinema. In 2011, he opened the curtains as a tapas bar (show starts at 6pm), its name derived from a backdrop from the 2007 film *Madrigal* that covers one wall (above). The beautifully lit bare bricks of the eclectic 1919 townhouse are decorated with artist Javier Guerra's revolutionary iconography, film posters and antiques. It's a natural home for the *farándula* – Havana's bobo thespian in-crowd. In the park up the road, a statue of John Lennon was unveiled in 2000 by Fidel in a 'Let It Be' gesture, 36 years after he banned The Beatles. Opposite is the Yellow Submarine Club, and, as an odd Brit-mania takes hold, island-impounded locals have adopted the Union Jack as street fashion. *Calle 17, 809 altos entre 2 y 4, T 831 2433*

Espacios

This late-night haunt makes a deal of its valet service, which, considering the wide, half-empty street outside and absence of crime in Cuba, is rather endearing. But in a way you can see why. This is tony Miramar, the only corner of this still-socialist country where there are cars to actually park. It's a novelty – much like the gourmet fast-food joint La Pachanga (T 830 2507), which got so rammed it built a VIP room. Espacios is far more than a glorified garage, of course. It's set in a mansion seemingly still lived in – arriving feels as if you're gatecrashing a fabulous house party. Multiple rooms are filled with art, antiques and quirky objects, and hefty helpings of tapas are served. But really it all happens after-hours in the back garden, where there's a bar, BBQ, tinkling fountain and films projected on to the wall. *Calle 10, 513 entre 5ta y 7ma, T 202 2921*

Río Mar
Not being commercially minded, Havana has few waterfront venues, so when this *paladar* opened in 2012 with a terrace by the river mouth it was on a promise. Río Mar backed it up with great seafood, frappé cocktails, a wine cellar and slick service. Rivalling the views are the glass chromatics, mosaic tiles and understated style of the 'private' room (pictured).
Avenida 3ra, 11 entre C y Final, T 209 4838

El Pedregal

Purpose-built in 1997 to target custom from western Havana's congress centre, institutes and embassies, El Pedregal means 'place of stones', and Joaquín Galván's design serenely fuses them with concrete, glass, wood and foliage, as well as terraces overlooking a manmade lake. The Cuban/international menu is relatively inexpensive – the diplomaterati splurge on fine wine and vintage liqueurs. Club nights on Saturdays feature artists of the calibre of Carlos Varela; there are also occasional gigs by the pool at hip grill La Campana (T 271 1073) down the road. Thirty years previously, Galván was one of the architects responsible for the nearby CNIC (Avenida 25 entre 21 y 21a), a madcap scientific research centre inspired by Byzantine galleys and Japanese brutalism. *Avenida 23 esq 198, T 273 7832*

La Casona de 17

It is claimed Castro's godparents used to live in the Grand House on 17, and you can imagine a bearded toddler outside this peach-coloured colonial house, organising his *compañeritos* into microbrigades. The restaurant has exquisite art deco lights, immaculate stucco and contemporary art, but is rather staid. Have a peek before settling into the BBQ area in the annexe, which buzzes with families and workers at lunch, who come for the excellent-value grills; afterwards, cross the road to La Torre (see p010), for views and digestifs. A Prado y Neptuno (T 860 9636) is another option for a quick bite (always a challenge in Cuba). It serves Italian staples within a contemporary space designed by Roberto Gottardi, joint architect of ENA (see p076), featuring pop art murals by Emilio Castro. *Calle 17, 60 entre M y N, T 838 3136*

Milano Lounge Club

Almost all the private houses designed by the top architects in the 1940s and 1950s are off-limits (see p064), hence our elation regarding the conversion of this 1946 Max Borges Recio residence. Its three white volumes are tied together by cantilevered balconies, horizontal black balustrades and French windows, calling to mind a sailing club. The sharp angles of the restaurant's monochrome interior are offset by sofas, wicker and a lovely garden. The executive chef worked in the Cuban embassy in Paris, and Italian and international dishes are beautifully presented. Indicative of the new entrepreneurial work ethic, Milano opens at breakfast, and at midnight tables are cleared for dancing until dawn. There's a South Beach vibe – no doubt a few of its privileged patrons have just flown in.
Avenida 3ra, 2404 entre 24 y 26, T 203 4641

Restaurante 1830

This supperclub complex, in a neoclassical mansion on a promontory at the mouth of the Almendares, is named after the year it was born. Interiors are part restored, part eclectic; original iron grilles, turn-of-last-century chairs, chandeliers and fireplaces, and art deco-style stained glass in the library, now Bar Colonial, which is a refined spot for a sharpener. A red carpet leads to an array of dining rooms, with a Cuban/

French menu and dishes such as prawns flambéed in rum. Sadly, the state-run establishment is often half-deserted, but right behind it is Los Jardines, which has a 'Japanese'-themed island covered in shells (don't ask) and draws lively crowds to events such as the Sunday salsa sessions. However, schedules aren't worth the paper they're written on in Cuba, so call ahead. *Malecón 1252 y 22, T 838 3090*

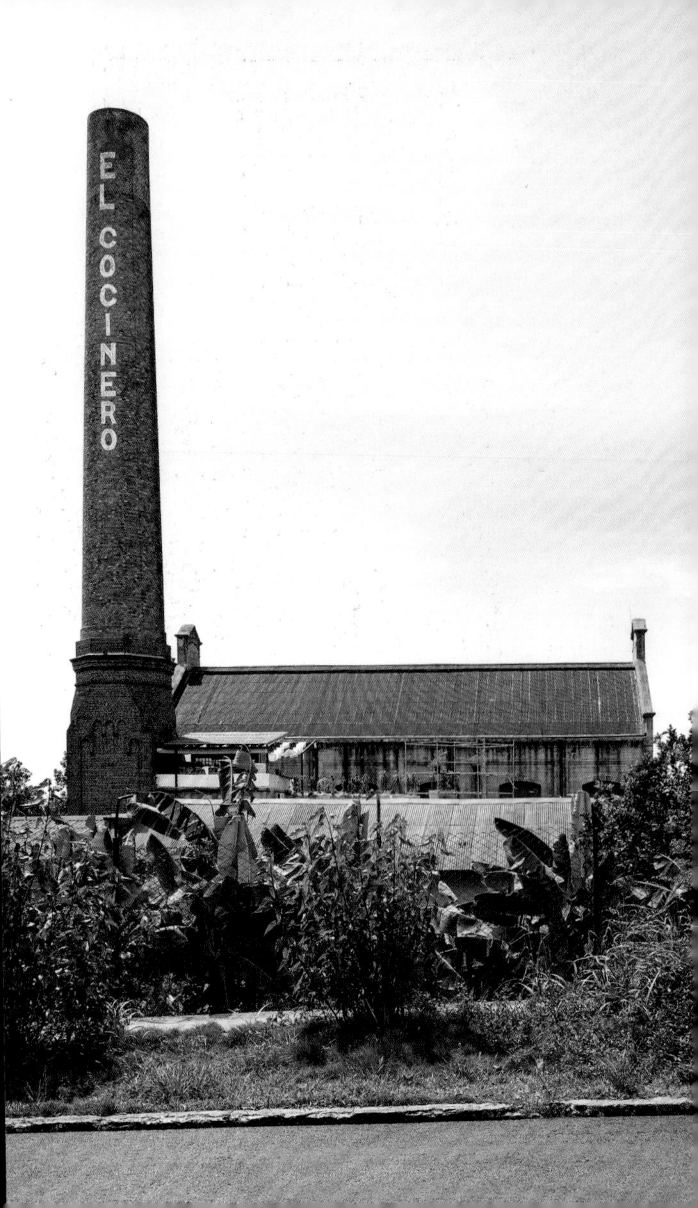
EL COCINERO

El Cocinero

Raúl's real-estate reforms and the tentative lease of state property are a lifeline for the city's threatened urban heritage, and a glorious opportunity, as manifested in this savvy loft conversion. The 1913 factory is known as El Cocinero after the peanut-oil company resident here in the 1930s. Up the spiral stairs of its (now uplit) 42m brick chimney, a loungey terrace has seating in stone alcoves and on repro Verner Pantons and BKFs, and a steel skeleton supports a shed-like bar; the more formal interior (above) is hung with art by Enrique Wong and Arlés del Río. Food (tuna tataki, baked camembert) and service are impeccable. The ambitious Fábrica de Arte Cubano (see p062) hosts galleries, gigs, films, plays and events within the industrial space below. *Calle 26 entre 11 y 13, T 832 2355, www.elcocinerohabana.com*

INSIDER'S GUIDE

EME ALFONSO, SINGER AND COMPOSER

Born into a musical dynasty, Eme Alfonso first recorded aged seven and is now a solo artist. She studied at ENA (see p076) and it brings back fond memories. 'The landscape, cupolas, labyrinths, ruins – it's an inspiration for thousands of artists who pass through,' she says.

In Habana Vieja, Alfonso loves the artisan design store Piscolabis (San Ignacio 75, T 5284 0355). She also recommends tapas joint El Chanchullero (Teniente Rey 457a, T 5276 0938), which is tiny but portions are not; the contemporary dance performances at Retazos (Amargura 61, T 860 4341); and, in restored Plaza Vieja, the micro-brewery Taberna de la Muralla (San Ignacio 368, T 866 4453): 'If the weather's hot, the beer hits the spot.' A regular at Teatro Bertolt Brecht (see p040), she is enthused about her brother X Alfonso's huge multidisciplinary project Fábrica de Arte Cubano (Calle 11 entre 24 y 26), which opened in late 2013 to provide a platform for emerging artists. And, of course, she watches baseball at El Latino (see p092). 'All the shouting and arguing is typical of my culture.'

Come the evening, she likes dining at Café Laurent (see p038) or El Cocinero (see p060) before heading to Espacios (see p053). 'It's frequented by artists and feels like the house of an old friend.' In her free time, Alfonso goes to the beach. 'When I'm on tour, I miss the salt on my lips,' she says. 'That, and the Cuban sense of humour. However bad the situation, someone will always crack a joke.'
For full addresses, see Resources.

ARCHITOUR
A GUIDE TO HAVANA'S ICONIC BUILDINGS

The city's architectural history is almost totally intact as urbanism has been stunted for nearly half a century, and economic necessity preserved outstanding stock that anywhere else would have been bulldozed for developers' greed or health-and-safety diktats. Many buildings have fallen down, but those that remain, including the neoclassical villas and flamboyant art deco mansions abandoned by the upper class, have been commandeered and divvied up into multi-family dwellings using screens and improvised mezzanines. Disappointingly, many of the best preserved houses, such as those designed by Mario Romañach and one by Richard Neutra, are now diplomatic residences ensconced on private roads in Cubanacán.

After the revolution, two-thirds of the country's architects left. The idealistic remained and remarkable projects were undertaken, such as the still-popular Habana del Este residential suburb and the Escuelas Nacionales de Arte (see p076), until the money ran dry and aesthetic austerity won out. Since then, development has been restricted to Soviet-style housing: faceless, prefab blocks in outlying suburbs and small-scale construction by microbrigades. Today, new builds are limited to hospitals and fledgling foreign investment (see p030). Meanwhile, bright revolutionary imagery remains an inescapable part of the urban fabric: slogans, mantras and images of Fidel and Che link public and private spaces.
For full addresses, see Resources.

Edificio Bacardí

The rum company left a glorious legacy when it fled Cuba in 1959. This 1930 art deco skyscraper by Esteban Rodríguez Castells, Rafael Fernández Ruenes and José Menéndez is grounded in red Bavarian granite, inlaid with brass, adorned with enamelled terracotta reliefs, including female nudes by Maxfield Parrish, and topped by the bat emblem. The exquisite entrance is swathed in veined, pastel marble and has a geometric sun-ray floor pattern, etched amber and opaque glass, stucco, cedar and mahogany panels. Head up to the eyrie for the 360-degree views before dusk, then sample a rum in the sumptuous maplewood-lined La Barrita (T 862 9310 ext 131; closes 9pm) above the main hall. Detail even extends to the toilet doors' gold leaf and intricate marquetry. *Monserrate 261 esq San Juan de Dios*

Club Náutico
An overlapping sequence of concrete shells, designed by Max Borges Recio in 1953, allows sunlight into a shaded, airy pavilion. Similar to Borges' earlier Tropicana (see p048), even down to the valets' canopy, Náutico is less wave-like, more giant sea cucumber. After the revolution, it became a club for civil servants. A visit requires a backhander.
Calle 152, Reparto Náutico

Museo de Artes Decorativas

José Gómez Mena invented the mall in Cuba and, with the profits, commissioned a villa from French architects Viard et Dastugue and interiors by Jansen in Paris. Finished in 1927, the 11 rooms lead off the balconied double-height vestibule (opposite), with its switchback stairs, skylight, Carrara marble and bronze- and gold-plated decorative ironwork. Mena's sister, a countess, threw society do's here, showing off the Sèvres,

Meissen and Wedgwood in the Regency dining room – witness the photos on the landing. The owners fled in 1961, stashing their worldly goods in the basement. The house was restored in 2003 and turned into a repository for decorative arts with some 35,000 pieces. Most interesting are the original rooms, notably the art deco bathroom with the tub built into an alcove. *Calle 17 esq E, T 830 9848*

Cementerio Cristóbal Colón

Havana's cemetery stretches for seven blocks in the centre of town, with its own street grid system and grand architecture, notably the 1936 mausoleum of Catalina Lasa and Juan Pedro Baró (above). French glass master René Lalique, who worked on the couple's Vedado house, Casa de la Amistad (T 830 3114), used Bergamo marble and onyx to fashion a minimalist white cupola, contrasting a black granite door engraved with two praying angels. As the first woman to get divorced in Latin America in 1918 (to be with Baró), Lasa was buried under 6m of concrete so as not to profane the neighbours. Another must-see is the Borges brothers' concrete, tent-shaped, 1957 Núñez-Gálvez tomb. The cemetery is also the resting place of musicians Rubén González and Ibrahim Ferrer and photographer Alberto Korda.

Edificio Solimar

Among the squat architectural hotchpotch and cultural meltdown of Centro rises the eight-storey pink-hued Solimar, dulled and weathered by its namesakes, the sun and the sea. Radical when built in 1944, Manuel Copado's poured-concrete block made fine use of an awkward plot, its stretched form maximising ventilation and light, but ultimately the effects of corrosion too. Overlooking the Malecón, its expressive, Mendelsohnian walkways evoke the view of the crashing waves. Centro's streets are a riot of art deco and art nouveau facades, although most are in a perilous state. Look up to spot rusting iron grillework, moulded cement bas-reliefs and stylised shopfront logos. You can rent a room in many of these historical gems, including Solimar (hang around below) although it's rather pokey. *Soledad 205 esq San Lázaro*

Casa de las Américas

The HQ of the most prestigious of Cuba's many cultural arms is an architectural hybrid – look closely to see the join. The private house was bought by the American Writers and Artists Association in 1947. An inscrutable volume was plonked on the third floor and Ramón del Busto added the telescopic tower in 1953, creating an ecclesiastical feel, uniting the ensemble with vertical shafts. There are art deco details in the relief map above the canopy entrance, the cupola and four-faced clock. The institution runs a publishing house and promotes Latin American literature and art. Galleries display work from the 1960s to the 1970s, there are rotating exhibitions and past speakers have included Mario Vargas Llosa and Gabriel García Márquez. *Avenida 3ra, 52 esq G, T 838 2706, www.casadelasamericas.org*

Edificio Girón

The location of this 17-storey concrete block comes as a surprise. A slab of Soviet brutalism incongruously overlooking the Caribbean, it has stood defiant since 1967, its presence accentuated by the lack of nearby tall buildings. From afar, this allows an appreciation of Antonio Quintana and Alberto Rodríguez's meticulous design: the parallel lines of the floating stairs, shielded by brise-soleil; the sky bridges; the Googie-style rocket 'feet'; the studs on the supporting walls. As you approach, you notice not only further detail, such as the organic steps of the plinth and the typeface of the Girón sign (the high-rise was named after the bus company that housed its employees here), but also the neglect, perhaps the reason many locals believe it is the ugliest building in Havana. *Malecón entre E y F*

Cine La Rampa

This former bowling alley was converted into a 1,000-seat cinema by hydraulically lifting the roof. Designed by Gustavo Botet in 1955, its internal ramp system is lined with brass banisters and classic Cuban film posters. The building houses the national archive yet shows mainly US and European films. You can't miss it for the huge retro logo on the side wall.
La Rampa entre O y P, T 878 6146

Escuelas Nacionales de Arte (ENA)

Fidel and Che played a round of golf at the old country club before ripping it up for the National Art Schools. Overseen by Ricardo Porro, work began with great optimism in 1961, reflected in the expressionism of the five projects: Ballet (opposite) and Music ('the worm', above) by Vittorio Garatti; Dramatic Arts by Roberto Gottardi, another Italian; and Fine Arts and Modern Dance by Cuban Porro, who took a sensual approach ('I made cupolas in the form of breasts'). A shortage of materials was a blessing as the brick and tile Catalan vaults suited the lush setting, but Soviet doctrine halted work in 1965 with only Porro's schools complete, although four remain in use. This magnum opus is at last being finished in consultation with Garatti, Gottardi and ballet dancer Carlos Acosta. Book a tour (CUC5) in town.
Calle 120, 1110 entre Avenida 9na y 13

Wall of Flags
In 2006, the States began broadcasting propaganda such as: '*How sad that all the people who know how to run this country are driving taxis*' from a huge LED screen in Harrison & Abramovitz's 1953 embassy (pictured). Castro retaliated by erecting 138 flags to block the messages. Obama pulled the plug, but the architectural stand-off remains as a symbol of Cuban-US relations at their most tragicomic.

SHOPPING
THE BEST RETAIL THERAPY AND WHAT TO BUY

Apart from those must-buys: cigars, rum, music and coffee, the city remains a retail vacuum. The restoration of the old town has resulted in the oddly unsettling arrival of Benetton and Adidas, and themed stores such as *perfumería* Habana 1791 (Mercaderes 156 esq Obrapía, T 861 3525), which creates bespoke scents. Lithograph prints (opposite), film posters (see p086) and revolutionary art are fascinating design-wise, and the commercial art spaces La Casona (Muralla 107 esq San Ignacio, T 863 4703) and Galería Habana (see p084) carry Cuba's foremost contemporary talent. Music shops abound, although the best-kept secrets are the Egrem pressings at Areito (see p047) and back-room vinyl in Seriosha (Neptuno 408).

Local fashion designers have been trying to coax *cubanas* out of spandex with contemporary takes on traditional dress. The most successful has been Jacqueline Fumero, and she now has a funky, eponymous Cafe & Boutique (Compostela 1 esq Cuarteles, T 862 6562). Alternatively, pick up a classic linen *guayabera* shirt from El Quitrín (Obispo esq San Ignacio, T 862 0810). La Maison (Calle 16 esq 7ma, T 204 1543) has a few stores in a 1946 villa, but the real draw is the courtyard catwalk show over dinner at weekends, often followed by a pool party. At the other end of the spectrum, the granting of retail licences to individuals has made it easier than ever to pick up bootleg CDs or a cheap sink flown in from Miami. *For full addresses, see Resources.*

Taller Experimental de Gráfica

In most other countries, the printing equipment in this workshop would either be on the scrap heap or in a museum. In Cuba, things don't work like that – witness the iconic 1950s cars, still running thanks to huge feats of ingenuity, such as using tights for fan belts (perhaps explaining all the flesh on show). The country has a strong graphic-design tradition, and while this warehouse – with its wobbly wooden desks, antiquated machinery and bare bulbs – resembles something from another era, the lithographs, woodcuts and copper and zinc engravings made are modern and often provocative, and its alumni have pieces in the Museo Nacional (see p033). Prints and collages are on sale, and courses in English cost 50CUC per day (or 150CUC per week). Open 10am to 4pm, weekdays. *Callejón del Chorro 62, T 864 6013*

La Moderna Poesía
Ricardo Mira and Miguel Rosich's stained-grey concrete art deco gorilla has sat territorially on its two columned fists at the bottom of Obispo since 1938. Inside is a basic interior stocked with a typically Cuban lucky dip. You'll find DVDs about Fidel, books on Afro-Cuban traditions, romantic salsa CDs, Sigourney Weaver biographies and a very well-stocked bar.
Bernaza 527 esq Obispo, T 861 6983

Galería Habana

There's an impeccable pedigree to this small but influential gallery, which has been exhibiting Cuba's finest artists since 1962 – it opened with Mariano Rodríguez, moved on to Wifredo Lam, and currently represents Manuel Mendive and Roberto Fabelo. It continues to operate from an incongruous location, an asymmetrical space at the bottom of a residential block, yet the eight thought-provoking shows each year remain essential viewing. Recent exhibitions have included Los Carpinteros' witty installations, Carlos Garaicoa's architectural statements, Roberto Diago's 'maroonage' (using found objects), Yoan Capote's sculptures and Tonel's cartoon- and text-based work ('Nada que Aprender', above). Also check out the large-scale visual art at Factoría Habana (T 864 9512). *Línea entre E y F, T 832 7101*

La Vajilla

By far your most rewarding buy in this city is genuine period furniture, although the red tape surrounding its exportation can be exhausting and the rules change all the time. South Americans in general are obsessed by the new; Cubans particularly so, due to their lack of exposure to the outside world. Hence the truckloads of antiques and covetables that arrive daily at this two-floored treasure trove, as art nouveau lamps, Cuban mahogany cabinets and 19th-century European glassware are unsentimentally thrown out in favour of modern kitsch. La Vajilla is an official shop, so everything has kosher paperwork. Prices seem high until it dawns they're in local pesos (£1 = MN45). Bargain, but don't lose focus – you have to get that marble tabletop home somehow.
Avenida de Italia 502 esq Zanja, T 862 4751

ICAIC

The antithesis of Hollywood's approach, post-revolution Cuban silk-screen film posters eschewed individual stars for a minimalist or pop art representation of the *obra* (work) itself. Classic images adorn every inch of the ICAIC foyer (pictured); the posters themselves, and DVDs of Cuban films, are sold across the road, through the back of the Fresa y Chocolate café.
Calle 23, 1155 entre 10 y 12, T 831 1101

SPORTS AND SPAS
WORK OUT, CHILL OUT OR JUST WATCH

In a country where daily life is a struggle, state-funded sport is free entertainment, as well as a welcome distraction – like those other legendary Cuban pastimes, sex and *jineterismo* (literally, riding tourists). This proud sporting nation punches way above its weight considering its backward training facilities. It has won 34 Olympic boxing golds, and rivalry with the US at baseball (see p092) is as keen as the ideological battle. Cubans also excel at basketball and volleyball – watch at the colourful Estadio Ramón Fonst (Avenida de la Independencia esq Bruzón, T 881 1011) or Kid Chocolate (see p090); fixtures are posted on boards outside and at www.inder.cu.

For something more sedate, make like Ernest and charter a boat at Marina Hemingway (Calle 248 esq 5ta, T 204 5088; CUC300 for four hours) to go deep-sea fishing for marlin, wahoo and tuna. No matter how dire the economy, locals will always dress to impress, and independent spas and beauty parlours, such as O2 (Calle 26, 5 esq 26b, T 883 1663), are a nascent cottage industry. The best pools are in the hotels, notably on the roof of Parque Central (see p016) and Saratoga (see p021), and at the Riviera (see p026), for its 1950s tiered diving boards. Or join the weekend exodus past the 1960s satellite town of Habana del Este to the party beaches of Playas del Este, 20km away. If you can ignore the odd oil rig, it's a more authentic experience than the island's sanitised resorts. *For full addresses, see Resources.*

Club Habana

Most of the city's original members-only beach and sports clubs, such as Náutico (see p066), were turned over to the unions after the revolution, but Habana somehow remains an exclusive domain of diplomats and expats. In its previous incarnation as the Havana Yacht Club, this place was so elitist that it declined President Batista's application because he was *mulato*. These days, it is open to all, or at least the few who can afford the CUC20 day rate, and consequently you can often have the place almost to yourself. Pass security and carry on up the drive to the Beaux Arts facade of Rafael Goyeneche's 1928 clubhouse. Laze by one of the pools or on the 500m private beach, use the gym, take a sauna or find out if anyone's for tennis. Then pad over to the BBQ for some grilled lobster. *Avenida 5ta entre 188 y 192, T 204 5700*

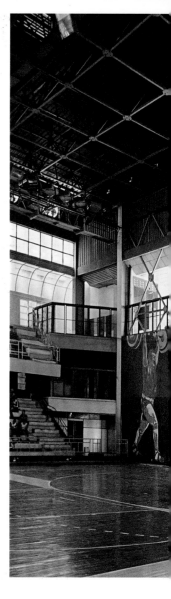

Sala Polivalente Kid Chocolate

This multi-use sports hall is named after
boxing hero Eligio 'Kid Chocolate' Sardiñas
(he was small and black; this was before
the days of PC), who became Cuba's first
world champion in 1931. As well as local
and national bouts, there's wrestling, judo,
basketball, five-a-side, badminton and
handball. Check the board outside (just
off Parque Central) and watch for a few
local pesos. The venue's dilapidated state
is masked by a typically colourful Cuban
interior and the shafts of sunlight that
poke through the painted glass and reflect
off the varnish. It might be atmospheric
but it doesn't exactly provide the best
conditions for top-level sport, although
at least the wooden floor lends a spring
to players' leaps. Four giant murals display
the rewards of perseverance in the face of
adversity – such as rain dripping through
the roof and regular power cuts.
Prado entre Brasil y San Martín, T 861 1546

Estadio Latinoamericano

Baseball was brought to Cuba in the 1860s by US dockers loading sugar in Matanzas. When the Spanish banned it in favour of bullfighting, the game became a symbol of defiance cemented in the national psyche. It remains wildly popular – bring a bat and you could start an innings in a parking lot (it's not hard to find one). El Latino opened in 1946 in working-class Cerro (before everywhere became working class) and is the Caribbean's largest ballpark – 60,000 saw Cuba beat the US here in 1961. Home to local team Industriales (the Blue Lions, hence the paint job), its concrete mesh allows ventilation, and laddered floodlights peer in at the action. Games are at 8pm (2pm Sundays) during the December to May season. It's all raucously good fun, often aided by smuggled-in rum.
Pedro Pérez 302, T 873 2527

Gimnasio Rafael Trejo

Sandwiched between blocks in the most tumbledown corner of colonial Havana, this simple open-air boxing ring under a corrugated-iron roof has fostered dreams of greatness (and escape) in eager boys since 1940. It's raw and primal, like the sport itself, yet El Trejo has produced a conveyor belt of Olympic champions from Mario Kindelán and Félix Savón to triple-gold medallist Teófilo Stevenson, who became an even greater national hero after a promoter tried to tempt him to defect in Munich in 1972 and he said: 'The only millions that interest me are the eight million Cubans.' Watch from the bleachers (Fridays, 7pm) or have a go yourself. Half a day's training costs CUC25 and you'll get first dibs on the solitary punchbag.
Cuba 815 entre Merced y Leonor Pérez, T 862 0266

ESCAPES

WHERE TO GO IF YOU WANT TO LEAVE TOWN

Many Cubans dream of escape but find it only in music and dance. However, the island itself is enchanting to explore, but don't try to do it in a rush as infrastructure is poor. The Soviet planes have a chilling safety record and although Cuba has the Caribbean's only railway, the train to Santiago, cheekily dubbed the Orient Express, takes 15 hours if you are lucky. At least José Antonio Choy's 1997 Gehry-like station, one of the country's only postmodern builds, provides a startling welcome. The 1950s Chevrolets and Buicks are photogenic but belch and splutter; for longer rides book an official air-con taxi; the three-hour trip to Viñales (see p102) costs CUC90.

Avoid the tourist apartheid at all-inclusive resorts like Varadero, which are about as Cuban as silence, so much so that a UK-financed gated golf resort here will offer foreigners a rare chance to buy property. Instead, combine sun worship with a trip to Cienfuegos (see p098) and Trinidad (see p100). Journey Latin America (12-13 Heathfield Terrace, London, T +44 20 8747 8315) can tailor-make an itinerary, including international flights, transport and a guide. Alternatively, hire a car and stray off the beaten path. Head to the northern cays, or to go scuba-diving way out west at Maria La Gorda – few road trips are as entertaining, especially if you enter into the socialist spirit and give the locals a lift. There's no traffic but beware of potholes, cows in the fast lane and migrating crabs. *For full addresses, see Resources.*

Finca La Vigía, San Francisco de Paula
Ernest Hemingway is revered in Cuba. But whether that's because he lived in Havana for 21 years and wrote three books here, most famously *The Old Man and the Sea*, or because he keeps the cash registers ringing, is hard to fathom. With that in mind, avoid the overhyped Bodeguita and El Floridita, where he used to drink, and head 15km into the suburbs to his house, which remains exactly as it was when he died in 1960. You're not allowed in but peer through the windows at his books, photos, hunting trophies and typewriter, and art by Picasso and Miró. In the grounds is his boat and the pool in which Ava Gardner took a dip. Have lunch at nearby Las Ruinas (T 643 1274), Joaquín Galván's clever 1972 reappropriation of a sugar mill in Parque Lenin, a relic of Soviet-Cuban ideals.
Calle Estinger y Vigía, T 691 0809

Cienfuegos

Friendships with Cubans in Havana can be infuriating as you can never determine if there's a hidden agenda (assume there is). However, in the provinces the warmth and curiosity of the locals is unaffected. Leafy, laidback Cienfuegos sits on a peninsula in a natural harbour. Founded in 1819, it was settled by immigrants from Bordeaux and the US French colonies, and its wide boulevards, neoclassical flamboyance and eclectic architecture portray the Gallic approach to urban planning. Built by the cane, the city boomed from 1890 to 1930. Sugar baron Acisclo del Valle brought craftsmen from Morocco to work on his neo-Moorish indulgence, the 1917 Palacio de Valle (T 4351 2891). He died two years later after commissioning another gem: the stately Yacht Club (right; T 4351 4441), of which he was president. Designed by Pablo Donato Carbonell, its inauguration in 1920 attracted the cream of society.

Trinidad

Founded in 1514 on Cuba's south coast, Trinidad was a dozy hamlet until the 18th century, when riches from the sugar trade began to flood in. At one stage, the Valle de los Ingenios was producing a third of the island's crop from 70 mills. Merchants and slave-trade plantation owners turned the city into the colonial jewel it is today, with its grandiose palaces, pastel-painted houses, stained glass and terracotta-tiled roofs, overseen by the 1813 bell tower (above) of the former San Francisco de Asís convent (opposite). Trinidad is six hours from Havana, so stay awhile. Spend your days on paradise island Cayo Blanco de Casilda, scuba-diving among turtles at its black coral reef, and nights at Disco Ayala, dancing among the stalactites in a beautifully lit cavern. Just watch out for the bats. And we're not talking Bacardí.

Valle de Viñales
The verdant karst landscape 160km
south-west of Havana is punctuated by
steep, flat-topped *mogote* mountains,
underground caverns and lakes, while
tobacco plantations here supply many
of Havana's cigar factories (see p037).
The pretty village of Viñales is sleepy by
day but the salsa kicks in at dusk. Chill
by the pool in Hotel Los Jazmines (T 4879
6205), overlooking the serene valley.

NOTES
SKETCHES AND MEMOS

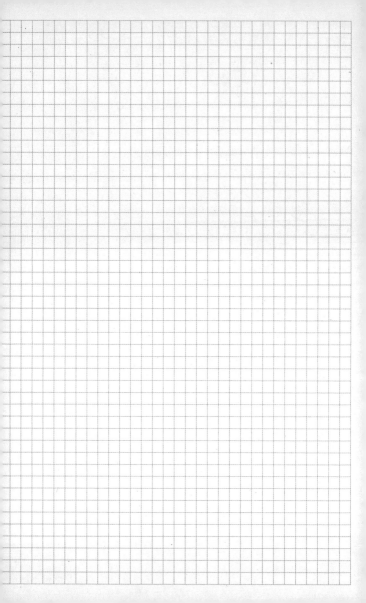

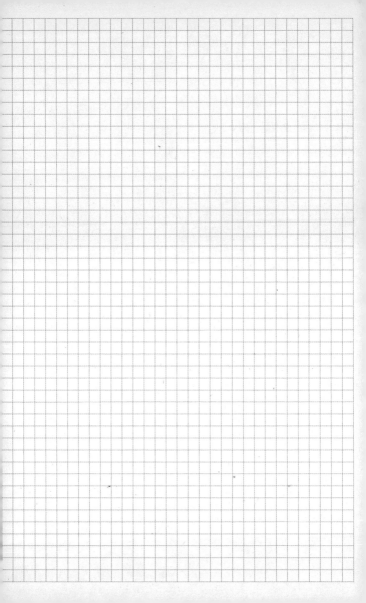

RESOURCES

CITY GUIDE DIRECTORY

HOTELS

ADDRESSES AND ROOM RATES

Artedel 024
Room rates:
double, from CUC60
T 830 8727
www.cubaguesthouse.com

Hotel Capri 016
Room rates:
prices on request
Calle 21 esq N
T 833 3747

Hotel Florida 029
Room rates:
double, CUC150;
Suite 18, CUC200
Obispo 252 esq Cuba
T 862 4127
www.hotelfloridahavana.com

Hostal Valencia 016
Room rates:
double, CUC150
Oficios 53 esq Obrapía
T 867 1037
www.habaguanexhotels.com

Hotel Los Jazmines 103
Room rates:
double, from CUC80
Carretera de Viñales
Valle de Viñales
T 4879 6205

Meliá Cohíba 016
Room rates:
double, from CUC280
Avenida Paseo entre 1ra y 3ra
T 833 3636
www.meliacuba.com

Hotel Nacional de Cuba 020
Room rates:
double, CUC175
Calle O esq 21
T 836 3564
www.hotelnacionaldecuba.com

Palacio del Marqués de San Felipe 017
Room rates:
double, CUC230;
suite, CUC350
Oficios 152 esq Amargura
T 864 9191
www.hotelmarquesdesanfelipe.com

Hotel Parque Central 016
Room rates:
double, CUC280
Neptuno esq Zulueta
T 860 6627
www.hotelparquecentral-cuba.com

Hotel Raquel 029
Room rates:
double, CUC150;
Junior Suite, CUC200
Amargura esq San Ignacio
T 860 8280
www.habaguanexhotels.com

Hotel Riviera 026
Room rates:
double, CUC110
Avenida Paseo y Malecón
T 836 4051
www.hotelhavanariviera.com

Hotel Santa Isabel 016
Room rates:
double, CUC280
Baratillo 9 entre Obispo y Narciso López
Plaza de Armas
T 860 8201
www.habaguanexhotels.com

Hotel Saratoga 021
Room rates:
double, from CUC230;
Junior Suite Saratoga, from CUC280;
Habana Suite, CUC710
Prado 603 esq Dragones
T 868 1000
www.hotel-saratoga.com

Hotel Terral 018
Room rates:
double, CUC150;
Junior Suite 401, CUC200
Malecón esq Lealtad
T 860 2100
www.habaguanexhotels.com

Torre Atlantic penthouses 030
Room rates:
penthouse, from CUC1,000
(three-night minimum stay)
T 833 0081
www.rentincuba.com

Tryp Habana Libre 028
Room rates:
double, CUC250
Calle L esq 23
T 834 6100
www.meliacuba.com

Villa María 024
Room rates:
double, CUC250;
villa, CUC700
T 362 0667
www.havanacasaparticular.com

WALLPAPER* CITY GUIDES

Executive Editor
Rachael Moloney

Author
Jeremy Case

Art Director
Loran Stosskopf
Art Editor
Eriko Shimazaki
Designer
Mayumi Hashimoto
Map Illustrator
Russell Bell

Photography Editor
Elisa Merlo
Assistant Photography Editor
Nabil Butt

Chief Sub-Editor
Nick Mee
Sub-Editor
Farah Shafiq

Editorial Assistant
Rodrigo Márquez

Interns
Rachel Hayek
Rebeca Plaza
Albert Sabás

Wallpaper* Group Editor-in-Chief
Tony Chambers
Publishing Director
Gord Ray
Managing Editor
Oliver Adamson

Wallpaper* ® is a
registered trademark
of IPC Media Limited

First published 2007
Revised and updated
2011 and 2014

All prices are correct at
the time of going to press,
but are subject to change.

Printed in China

PHAIDON

Phaidon Press Limited
Regent's Wharf
All Saints Street
London N1 9PA

Phaidon Press Inc
180 Varick Street
New York, NY 10014

Phaidon® is a registered
trademark of Phaidon
Press Limited

www.phaidon.com

A CIP Catalogue record for
this book is available from
the British Library.

ISBN 978 0 7148 6655 0

PHOTOGRAPHERS

RGBStudio/Alamy
Finca La Vigía, p097

Jerónimo Álvarez
Eme Alfonso, p063

Gianni Basso
Coppelia, p039

Alejandro Cartagena González
Havana city view, inside front cover
Edificio FOCSA, p010
Palacio del Marqués de San Felipe, p017
Hotel Terral, p018, p019
Hotel Nacional de Cuba, p020
Hotel Saratoga, p021, pp022-023
Villa María, p024, p025
Tryp Habana Libre, p028
Hotel Florida, p029
Torre Atlantic penthouses, p030, p031
Museo Nacional de Bellas Artes, p033
Museo de la Revolución, p034
Real Fábrica de Tabacos Partagás, p035
Café Laurent, p038
Teatro Bertolt Brecht, p040, p041
Malecón, pp044-045

Casa Miglis, p046
Atelier, p049
Le Chansonnier, p050, p051
Café Madrigal, p052
Espacios, p053
Río Mar, pp054-055
La Casona de 17, p057
Milano Lounge Club, p058
Restaurante 1830, p059
El Cocinero, p060, p061
Museo de Artes Decorativas, p068, p069
Casa de las Américas, p072
Edifico Girón, p073
Taller Experimental de Gráfica, p081
Galería Habana, p084
La Vajilla, p085
Estadio Latinoamericano, p092, p093

Hans Engels
Edificio Bacardí, p065
Edificio Solimar, p071
La Moderna Poesía, pp082-083

Baldomero Fernandez
Embajada de Rusia, p011
Ministerio del Interior, pp012-013
Hospital Hermanos Ameijeiras, p014
Memorial José Martí, p015
Hotel Riviera, pp026-027
Callejón de Hamel, pp036-037

Casa de la Música Galiano, p047
El Pedregal, p056
Club Náutico, pp066-067
Cementerio Cristóbal Colón, p070
Cine La Rampa, pp074-075
Wall of Flags, pp078-079
ICAIC, pp086-087
Club Habana, p089
Sala Polivalente Kid Chocolate, pp090-091
Gimnasio Rafael Trejo, pp094-095

Tommy Huynh
Cienfuegos, pp098-099

John A Loomis
Escuelas Nacionales de Arte, p076, p077

Dia/Mediacolors
Valle de Viñales, pp102-103

Walter Bibikow/Age Fotostock/SuperStock
Plaza de la Catedral, pp042-043
Trinidad, p100

Designpics/SuperStock
Trinidad, p101

HAVANA

A COLOUR-CODED GUIDE TO THE HOT 'HOODS

PLAZA DE LA REVOLUCIÓN
One million Cubans would often squeeze into this symbolic square for a Fidel monologue

MIRAMAR
Boulevards are lined with mansions housing embassies, 'dollar' shops and restaurants

HABANA VIEJA
The colonial core has more than 4,000 listed buildings, ranging from baroque to art deco

LA RAMPA
This street is a non-stop strip of classic hotels and cinemas, fast-food joints and nightclubs

VEDADO
Neoclassical villas and modernist towers are interspersed with cultural centres and parks

CENTRO
The art nouveau gems here have seen better days but that somehow adds to their charm

For a full description of each neighbourhood, see the Introduction.
Featured venues are colour-coded, according to the district in which they are located.